It's All About the Heart

Bisi Oladipupo

Springs of life publishing

Contents

To Jesus Christ my Lord and saviour; to Him alone that laid down His life that I might have life eternal. To Him that lead captivity captive and gave gifts unto men (Ephesians 4; 8). One of those gifts is writing!.

Why The Heart?

Our hearts are so important and it is quite amazing that not much is said about them. The Bible tells us to keep our hearts with all diligence for a reason.

"Keep thy heart with all diligence; for out of it are the issues of life." (Proverbs 4:23).

It would have been good enough if the scriptures tell us to "keep our hearts with diligence" but it says "keep your heart with ALL diligence". In other words, we must not be negligent when it comes to issues of our hearts.

To keep this in context, it simply means we must guard what affects our hearts. We also need to protect our hearts from things that can hurt them.

Could this be a reason why the Bible says, "Abstain from all appearance of evil" (1 Thess 5:22). Notice that you do not need to go and taste to see if it is evil. Once it has the appearance of evil, we are told to flee from it.

IT'S ALL ABOUT THE HEART

The heart is the seat of our belief system (Romans 10:10), so we must be very careful about what we expose our hearts to.

In addition to that, God looks at the heart while men look at outward appearance. This was the criterion used when David was chosen as king as recorded in (1 Samuel 16: 7).

Did you know that the motives of our hearts will be judged? (1 Corinthians 4:5).

This book will look at different types of hearts, lessons from some people in the Bible, the importance of having and maintaining a tender heart, warnings about the heart, and much more.

Happy reading and do enjoy this wonderful moment!

Chapter One

What Really Makes a Person?

D id you know that what really makes a person is the state of their heart? Could this be why the Bible says that "As a man thinks in his heart, so is he"? If a person's heart is not with you, they may be with you physically but they are really not with you.

"For as he thinks in his heart, so is he. "*Eat and drink!*" *he says to you,* ***But his heart is not with you.***" (Proverbs 23:7).

In the earthly ministry of our Lord Jesus Christ, He said a few things about the heart.

"Do you not yet understand that whatever enters the mouth goes into the stomach and is eliminated? **18** But those things which proceed out of the mouth come from the heart, and they defile a man." (Matthew 15:17-18).

When God was looking to choose a man to be the king of Israel, the Lord looked for a man after His own heart (Acts 13: 22). Samuel almost missed it had the Lord not corrected him that He the Lord looks at the heart (1 Samuel 16: 7).

As a matter of fact, to show the priority the Lord placed on the heart, He actually looks to and fro the whole earth to show Himself strong towards them whose heart is perfect towards Him (2 Chronicles 16:9).

The heart is the seat of believing (Romans 10:10) and our attitudes and decisions come from the heart (Proverbs 23:7).

There is a reason why the Bible tells us that "out of the abundance of the heart the mouth speaks" (Matthew 12:34). It simply means that you can locate the heart of a person by what they say.

As we have seen that the heart is so important, we will look into the scriptures and learn more about the heart.

But someone said, I am born again. Do I need to attend to my heart?

Yes, we all do, otherwise, the Lord would not give us instructions about the heart. One good example is: "be tendered-hearted" (Ephesians 4: 32) and "love others with a pure heart" (1 Peter 1: 22).

Let us have a further look at the scriptures.

Chapter Two

Functions of the Heart

The Seat of Believing

The heart as we have mentioned earlier is the seat of believing. It is with the heart that a man believes unto righteousness (Romans 10: 9-10); this is one reason we need to be meditating on the Word of God.

We need to be intentional about what we apply our hearts to. In other words, what we focus on and give attention to will sooner or later affect us.

It is safe to say that a person first backslides in their heart before actions follow (Proverbs 14:14).

This is why we are told to abstain from all appearances of evil (1 Thess 5:22). We don't want to expose ourselves to negative things that do not line up with God's truth. We want to stay clear of those things.

"Apply thine heart unto instruction, and thine ears to the words of knowledge" (Proverbs 23: 12).

Trusting God is an Act of the Heart

It is with our hearts that we trust God.

"Trust in the Lord with all thine heart; and lean not unto thine own understanding" (Proverbs 3: 5).

We see in the book of Psalms where the psalmist speaks about trusting God with the heart (Psalms 112:7; Psalms 28:7).

The Heart Can Rejoice

Have you ever read scripture and suddenly you get revelation and your heart rejoiced? The scriptures say that the light of the eyes makes the heart rejoice (Proverbs 15:30).

Hannah's heart rejoiced when after God gave her a child (1Samuel 2:1). Good news can cause the heart to rejoice.

Our Heart is the Table For God's Word

The Bible tells us to write God's Word upon the table of our hearts (Proverbs 3:3). The more of God's Word we have in our hearts, the more opportunity we will give His Word to be manifested in our lives. The Bible tells us to let the Word of Christ dwell in us richly (Colossians 3:16).

Under the New Covenant, the Lord said in His Word that He would put His laws in our hearts.

"This is the covenant that I will make with them after those days, saith the Lord, I will put my laws into their hearts, and in their minds will I write them" (Hebrews 10:16).

When you look at the parable of the Sower, which should really be the parable of the soils if you look at the content, the Bible makes it clear that it is the heart that receives the Word of God (Mark 4: 15).

We Love God with Our Hearts

The Bible tells us to love the Lord our God with all our hearts:

"And you shall love the Lord your God with all your heart, with all your soul, with all your mind, and with all your strength" (Mark 12: 30).

The scriptures also tell us that God's love has been shed abroad in our hearts by the Holy Spirit given to us (Romans 5:5).

Therefore, the believer in Christ has what it takes to love God.

Affects the Outcome of Our Lives

It's rather unfortunate that not much emphasis is said about the heart bearing in mind the importance of our hearts.

There is a reason why the Bible tells us to "guard our hearts with all diligence".

"Keep thy heart with all diligence; for out of it are the issues of life" (Proverbs 4:23).

Our hearts are so important that we are told to keep them not just with diligence but "all diligence".

Another scripture tells us that as we think in our hearts so shall we be (Proverbs 23:7).

Understanding is of the Heart

True understanding is of the heart. This truth can be seen in the scripture below:

"Therefore they could not believe, because Isaiah said again:

"He has blinded their eyes and hardened their hearts, Lest they should see with *their* eyes, Lest they should understand with *their* hearts and turn, So that I should heal them." (John 12:39-40).

It is what we understand with our hearts that we will be able to apply to our lives. It is not enough to hear, but we must understand.

From the parable of the sower, only those that understood brought forth fruit.

"But he who received seed on the good ground is he who hears the word and understands *it,* who indeed bears fruit and produces: some a hundredfold, some sixty, some thirty." (Matthew 13: 23).

It is the Heart that Discerns

This is very clear in scripture:

Have you ever had a gut feeling about something in your heart? Could it be your heart warning you?

"He who keeps his command will experience nothing harmful; And a wise man's heart []discerns both time and judgment" (Eccl 8:5).

"Whoever keeps and observes a royal command will experience neither trouble nor misery; For a wise heart will know the []proper time and [appropriate] procedure" (Eccl 8:5 AMP).

We Forgive from the Heart

From scripture, we are told to forgive others as Christ also forgave us (Colossians 3:13).

In the gospels, the Lord taught us about forgiveness and how we need to forgive others. The account can be found in (Mathew 18:21-35).

The part of this account makes it clear that forgiveness must be done from the heart:

"So My heavenly Father also will do to you if each of you, **from his heart, does not forgive his brother** []his trespasses." (Matthew 18:35).

Strong Decisions Are Made from the Heart

When a firm decision is made from the heart, the person will likely stand by it.

In the Book of Daniel, the Bible tells us that Daniel "purposed in his heart that he would not defile himself with the portion of the king's meat nor wine" (Daniel 1:8).

So, we can see here that Daniel's decision was from the heart and this is how quality decisions are made.

Chapter Three

Different Types of Hearts

N ow that we know some functions of the heart, let us look at different types of hearts from scripture.

A Wise Heart

"My son, if your heart is wise, My heart will rejoice—indeed, I myself; Yes, my ⌷inmost being will rejoiceWhen your lips speak right things." (Proverbs 23:15-16).

Why would this person rejoice if their son's heart was wise? It's simply because good actions and decisions will flow out of a wise heart.

I have a friend that is always full of wisdom, indeed I can say that she has a wise heart.

A person with a wise heart will be called prudent and will be careful with their words (Proverbs 16: 21, 23).

Being prudent is the product of a wise heart.

A wise heart is also an indication of wisdom (Exodus 28:3).

A Pure Heart

A person with a pure heart does not mean that they will not make mistakes or have shortfalls, it simply means that their motives are pure.

A person with a pure heart sometimes may appear as being gullible, because they can see all things pure (Titus 1:15). They don't read meanings into things which sometimes means they can be caught off guard.

A pure heart will enhance intimacy with God (Psalms 24:3-2; Matthew 5:8; Proverbs 22:11).

We are to call upon the Lord with a pure heart (2 Timothy 2:22). The Lord knows everything, so we may as well be open to the Lord.

The Scriptures also tell us to love one another fervently with a pure heart (1Peter 1: 22). When we love one another with a pure heart, we will not have wrong motives. And when we do things for other people, we will not expect anything back from them. Our motives will be pure when we relate to others.

Proud Heart

The Bible also tells us that a person can have a proud heart. Pride is one thing amongst other things that the Lord hates (Proverbs 6:16-17).

The scriptures also tell us that a prideful person in the heart is an abomination to the Lord (Proverbs 16:5). The word "abomination" is a strong word; it means detest.

"The Lord detests the proud; they will surely be punished." (Proverbs 16:5 NLT).

So, why would a proud person be punished? It is because they are likely to refuse to humble themselves and ask for mercy; they are always right and refuse to be corrected. While the Lord delights in mercy, we need to position ourselves and ask for mercy (Hebrews 4:16).

This is one reason we must guard our hearts and ensure that our hearts are tender.

As Christians, we have an added advantage in that God's love has been poured out in our hearts by the Holy Spirit (Romans 5: 5). Therefore, we can resist pride and yield to God's love already in our hearts. In addition to that, the Bible says that we are dead to sin and should live unto righteousness (1 Peter 2:24).

A Meek Heart

Could there be a reason why the Lord was able to work through Moses very mightily?

(Now the man Moses was very meek, above all the men which were upon the face of the earth.) (Numbers 12:3 KJV).

According to the scripture above, Moses was the meekest man among all men on the face of the earth. That is simply amazing. Not the meekest man in his country, but above all men on the face of the earth.

Once again, we can see that what really matters is the heart and God looks at the heart. For those that are familiar with the life of Moses, he was not perfect but he had a meek heart.

Have you been taken advantage of because you have a meek heart? Just forgive and leave the matter to the Lord. Your priority is to protect your heart and ensure that it remains meek.

There are not many things stated in scripture that are of great price in the eyes of the Lord, however, a quiet and meek spirit is.

*"But let it be the hidden man of the heart, in that which is not corruptible, even the ornament **of a meek and quiet spirit, which is in the sight of God of great price**"* (1 Peter 3:4 KJV).

If a meek spirit is of great price in the sight of God, such a heart must be precious in the sight of the Lord.

Our Lord Jesus Christ is described as meek and lowly in heart (Matthew 11:29).

Therefore, having a meek heart is having the heart of Jesus Christ our Lord.

Tender Heart

Being tender is not automatic, otherwise, there would be no reason for the scriptures to tell us to be tenderhearted.

"And be kind to one another, tenderhearted, forgiving one another, even as God in Christ forgave you." (Ephesians 4:32).

A person with a tender heart will find it easy to forgive others. If you notice the statement that follows the phrase "tenderhearted" says "forgiving one another as Christ has forgiven us".

Having a tender heart does not mean that one will not do anything wrong. It simply means that such a person will repent quickly and know when something you have done is wrong. A tenderhearted in-dividual feels remorseful immediately after they realized doing wrong.

When David found Saul his enemy and cut part of his clothing off. The Bible tells us that David's heart smote him (1 Samuel 24:5). This is an indication of a tender heart.

God also promised Josiah that he would not see evil in his days because his heart was tender (2 Kings 2:19).

We have a closer look at the tender heart in another chapter.

Hardened Heart

Can a Christian have a hardened heart?

While the answer is yes, we have been instructed to have tender hearts (Ephesians 4:32).

Jesus Christ our Lord rebuked His disciples for having hardened hearts (Mark 8:17) and in the book of Hebrews we are told not to harden our hearts (Hebrews 3:13).

There are various levels of hardness of the heart.

Hardening of the heart is a process of a person refusing to respond to promptings or apply their heart to correction and act accordingly.

"Happy *is* the man who is always reverent, But he who hardens his heart will fall into calamity." (Proverbs 28:14).

Notice the phrase "hardens his heart". This indicates that it is a process.

We will have a closer look at a hardened heart a bit later.

A Merry Heart

The state of a person's heart will affect their countenance (Proverbs 15:13) and the Bible also tells us that a merry heart is as good as medicine (Proverbs 17:22).

An Upright Heart

An upright heart is a true and honest heart.

There are many blessings for those that have a true and honest heart.

Solomon's throne would have been established if he had a true and honest heart like David's his father's heart.

"*3 The Lord told him, "I have heard your prayer and supplication which you have made before Me; I have consecrated this house which you have built by putting My Name and My Presence there forever. My eyes and My heart shall be there perpetually. 4 **As for you, if you walk (live your life) before Me, as David your father walked, in integrity of heart and in uprightness, acting in accordance with everything that I have commanded you, and will keep My statutes and My precepts,** 5 then I will establish the throne of your kingdom over Israel forever, just as I promised your father David,* *saying, 'You shall not be without a man (descendant) on the throne of Israel." (1 Kings 9:3-5).' AMP).*

So, Solomon's throne could have been established if he had walked before the Lord with integrity of heart and uprightness and done all that the Lord had told him to do.

The intentions of our hearts are very important. The Lord searches and tries the hearts.

"I the Lord search the heart, I try the reins, even to give every man according to his ways, and according to the fruit of his doings."(Jeremiah 17:10 KJV).

Are the intentions of our hearts still important under the New Covenant? Yes, very much so. And if anything, we have a greater standard because Christ now lives in us (Colossians 1:27); we are dead to sin (1 Peter 2:24).

The love of God has been poured into our hearts, therefore, all we need to do is to yield unto righteousness.

The scripture also tells us that the intentions of our hearts will be judged.

"Therefore judge nothing before the time, until the Lord comes, who will both bring to light the hidden things of darkness and reveal the [] counsels of the hearts. Then each one's praise will come from God." (1 Corinthians 4:5).

A Fixed Heart

To live a vibrant Christian life, our hearts must be fixed on the Lord. We will look at "our hearts and our walk with the Lord" in another chapter.

David made it clear that his heart was fixed on the Lord (Psalms 57:7).

An Established Heart

When a person's heart is established in the grace of God through Jesus Christ, such a person will not be moved by strange doctrines.

In the book of Hebrews, the Bible is telling us to ensure that our hearts are established in the grace of God.

"Do not be carried []about with various and strange doctrines. For *it is* good that the heart be established by grace, not with foods which have not profited those who have been occupied with them." (Hebrews 13:9).

Our hearts also can be established before God the Father, blameless and in holiness.

"And may the Lord make you increase and abound in love to one another and to all, just as we *do* to you, [13] so that He may establish your hearts blameless in holiness before our God and Father at the coming of our Lord Jesus Christ with all His saints." (1 Thess 3:12-13).

A Deceived Heart

My prayer is that no one reading this book has this type of heart. The root cause of this is believing lies.

It is only the truth that can set anyone free:

"And you shall know the truth, and the truth shall make you free." (John 8:32).

Jesus is the only way to God (John 14: 6) anything apart from that is deception.

Every knee shall bow and every tongue will confess that Jesus Christ is Lord (Romans 14:11).

If you know anyone that thinks otherwise, you need to pray for them that they might encounter the truth.

In the book of Isaiah, the Lord narrates a carpenter that breaks down cedars, burns some to warm himself, bakes some, and then bows down to the rest and calls it a god.

The scripture further tells us that this person considers not in his heart what he has done and how such a person can believe the rest of the wood is a god. The full account can be found in (Isaiah 44:13-21).

The conclusion is that the person has a deceived heart.

"**He** feeds on ashes; A deceived heart has turned him aside; And he cannot deliver his soul, Nor say, "*Is there* not a lie in my right hand?" (Isaiah 44:20).

Not receiving the love of the truth can open up a person to deception.

A Sound Heart

The Bible tells us that a sound heart is the life of the flesh.

"A sound heart *is* life to the body, But envy *is* rottenness to the bones." (Proverbs 14:30).

"A calm *and* peaceful *and* tranquil heart is life *and* health to the body, But passion *and* envy are like rottenness to the bones" (Proverbs 14:30 AMP).

This is one reason why we need to meditate on the word of God and allow the peace of God to rule in our hearts (Colossians 3:15).

Chapter Four

Examples of Different Types of Hearts Seen in Individuals in the Bible

Jesus Christ

Our Lord Jesus Christ is calling us to learn of Him. And the question is to Learn what? Amongst others things, we are to learn His heart.

"Take my yoke upon you, and learn of me; for I am meek and lowly in heart: and ye shall find rest unto your souls." (Matthew 11:29 KJV).

The state of our hearts affects our souls. Notice the conjunction above "and ye shall find rest unto your souls.

Jesus Christ is our example, and we need to learn from Him.

David

David was described as a man after God's own heart (Acts 13:22) and the Lord had to look for Him (1 Samuel 13:14).

Was David a perfect man? No, he was not, but when David did wrong, he was quick to repent. When he sinned against the Lord in the case of Bathsheba, after Nathan the prophet told him what he did was not pleasing in the eye of the Lord, David gave no excuses but repented (2 Samuel 12:13). It is said that Psalms 51 was written by David in response to his sin.

Let us look at a few of these verses in Psalms 51.

"Have mercy upon me, O God, According to Your lovingkindness; According to the multitude of Your tender mercies, Blot out my transgressions. Wash me thoroughly from my iniquity, And cleanse me from my sin.

For I acknowledge my transgressions, And my sin is always before me. Against You, You only, have I sinned, And done this evil in Your sight—That You may be found just [ ]when You speak, And blameless when You judge." (Psalms 51:1-4).

We can see the heart cry of David in this Psalm. This is a fruit of a tender heart. Yes, David yielded to his flesh but he did humble himself and repent, that is the key to the mercy of God.

We can also see when David had an opportunity to kill Saul and he did not. David cut off a bit of Saul's cloth, however, the Bible tells us that David's heart troubled him.

"**4** *Then the men of David said to him, "This is the day of which the Lord said to you, 'Behold, I will deliver your enemy into your hand, that you may do to him as it seems good to you.'" And David arose and secretly cut off a corner of Saul's robe.* **5** *Now it happened afterward that David's heart troubled him because he had cut Saul's robe.*" (1 Samuel 24:4-5).

Another translation of the Bible reads, "*But then David's conscience began bothering him because he had cut Saul's robe.*"(1 Samuel 24:5 NLT).

A person with a tender heart will know when they have done something wrong and will repent. No excuses!

David always ensured that his heart was right. We can see this echoed in some of his Psalms.

"**23** *Search me, O God, and know my heart: try me, and know my thoughts:* **24** *And see if there be any wicked way in me, and lead me in the way everlasting.*" (Psalms 139:23-24 KJV).

David prayed this prayer because he took care of his heart.

Here, we see God instructing Solomon. We can see clearly God describing the heart of David:

"*4 Now if you walk before Me **as your father David walked, in integrity of heart and in uprightness,** to do according to all that I have commanded you, and if you keep My statutes and My judgments, 5 then I will establish the throne of your kingdom over Israel forever, as I promised David your father, saying, 'You shall not fail to have a man on the throne of Israel.'* (1 Kings 9:4-5).

Paul

We can see from scripture that Paul made a conscious effort to make sure that his heart was right.

"*I have hope in God, which they themselves also accept, that there will be a resurrection [] of the dead, both of the just and the unjust. This being so, I myself always strive to have a conscience without offense toward God and men.*" (Acts 24:15-16).

Paul is saying here that he makes sure he does not hold offense in his heart towards both God and men.

Paul knew the character of God and also walked in love with men. The only way Paul could have not had the offense in his heart towards men was to walk in love and be forgiving.

Could this be one reason the Lord was able to work through Paul and he wrote most of the New Testament?

Abraham

Many of us have heard about Abraham. He is called "The Father of us all" (Romans 4:16).

God made a covenant with Abraham and God blessed the earth through Abraham's seed (Genesis 22:18).

Did you know that one main reason that the Lord made such a covenant with Abraham was because of his heart? The Lord must have known that when He instructed Abraham to sacrifice his only son which was a test (Genesis 22:1-16), he would obey.

"You are the Lord God, Who chose Abram, And brought him out of Ur of the Chaldeans, And gave him the name Abraham; **You found his heart faithful before You,** *And made a covenant with him To give the land of the Canaanites, The Hittites, the Amorites, The Perizzites, the Jebusites, And the Girgashites—To give it to his descendants. You have performed Your words, For You are righteous."* (Nehemiah 9:7-8).

God found Abraham's heart faithful before Him.

"For the eyes of the Lord run to and fro throughout the whole earth, to show Himself strong on behalf of those whose heart is loyal to Him." (2 Chronicles 16: 9).

Moses

We mentioned Moses briefly when we spoke about a meek heart.

It is evident that Moses was very meek from the testimony written about him.

(Now the man Moses was very meek, above all the men which were upon the face of the earth.) (Numbers 12:3 KJV).

When you look at the interactions of Moses when he was provoked, in most cases he would just fall upon his face.

When the son of Korah and others rose up against Moses, his response was to fall upon his face. This account can be found in (Numbers 16: 1-4).

When the judgment of God came upon the men, Moses and this time Aaron they both fell upon their faces and pleaded with God.

"And the Lord spoke to Moses and Aaron, saying, 21 "Separate yourselves from among this congregation, that I may consume them in a moment." 22 Then they fell[] on their faces, and said, "O God, the God of the spirits of all flesh, shall one man sin, and You be angry with all the congregation"? (Numbers 16: 20-22).

Many times you find where Moses pleaded or prayed for the people (Numbers 14: 11-20; Numbers 21:7).

Moses did care for the people the Lord committed into his hands. This shows the great heart that Moses had.

Peter

Many of us are aware that Peter denied the Lord three times when he was put under pressure (Matthew 26:69 -75) which is safe to say was out of fear. One reason we can say this is because further down in scripture during Paul's ministry, he was rebuked for refusing to eat with Gentiles for fear of circumcision (Galatians 2:11-13).

After all the other disciples fled and left Jesus, Peter followed afar off (Matthew 26:56-58). In addition to that, Peter was the one who cut off the servant's ear that was part of the crowd that arrested Jesus (John 18: 4-10). Peter obviously loved the Lord.

We can see this in his response:

"And Peter remembered the word of Jesus who had said to him, "Before the rooster crows, you will deny Me three times." So he went out and wept bitterly." (Matthew 26:75).

Peter did not just weep, but he wept bitterly. The description of Peters weeping speaks volumes. Peter had a good heart and loved the Lord, however, he just missed it on this occasion.

Yes, he missed it, but he had an upright heart.

Having an upright heart does not mean that one will not miss it. It simply means, such a person will acknowledge when they are wrong and repent.

Judas Iscariot

It is safe to say that Judas Iscariot's real problem was a heart problem. This is quite serious considering the opportunities that Judas had to adjust and make changes in his heart.

Judas witnessed miracles (Matthew 10:1; Mark 8:19) and he listened to Jesus Christ teach and preach (Mark 4:10; Mark 9:35; Mark 10:32; Luke 8:1).

Judas obviously had lots of opportunities to readjust his heart but he did not.

At some point during the ministry of Jesus Christ on earth, this is what our Lord said about Judas Iscariot:

"Jesus answered them, "Did I not choose you, the twelve, and one of you is a devil?" He spoke of Judas Iscariot, the son of Simon, for it was he who would betray Him, being one of the twelve." (John 6: 70-71).

There is a reason why the Bible says that the greatest is love (1 Corinthians 13:13).

According to scripture, God's love has been poured into our hearts by the Holy Spirit (Romans 5: 5).

The first priority of every believer is to walk and stay in love (1 John 3:14).

"We love him, because he first loved us." (1 John 4:19).

We are to keep ourselves in the love of God (Jude 1:21).

A Man Called Simon

There is an account in the book of Acts about a man called Simon. This is how the Bible starts describing him:

"But there was a certain man called Simon, who previously practiced []sorcery in the city and astonished the []people of Samaria, claiming that he was someone great." (Acts 8: 9).

The account further tells us that after Philip preached, Simon himself believed and was baptized. The apostles at Jerusalem then sent Peter and John down to Samaria and they prayed for the new believers that they might receive the Holy Spirit (Acts 8: 14-17).

When Simon saw that through the laying on of hands, the Holy Spirit was received by the new believers, Simon offered money to Peter and John.

*"And when Simon saw that through the laying on of the apostles' hands the Holy Spirit was given, he offered them money, 19 saying, "Give me this power also, that anyone on whom I lay hands may receive the Holy Spirit." 20 But Peter said to him, "Your money perish with you, because you thought that the gift of God could be purchased with money! 21 You have neither part nor portion in this matter, **for your heart is not right in the sight of God. 22 Repent therefore of this your wickedness, and pray God if perhaps the thought of your heart may be forgiven you.** 23 For I see that you are poisoned by bitterness and bound by iniquity." 24 Then Simon answered and said, "Pray to*

the Lord for me, that none of the things which you have spoken may come upon me." (Acts 8:18-24 KJV).

Simon did this because his heart was not right with God and Peter addressed this.

Absalom

Absalom who brought David great grief and eventually lost his life was beautiful on the outside.

*"**Now in all Israel there was no one who was praised as much as Absalom for his good looks**. From the sole of his foot to the crown of his head there was no blemish in him. And when he cut the hair of his head—at the end of every year he cut it because it was heavy on him—when he cut it, he weighed the hair of his head at two hundred shekels according to the king's standard."* (2 Samuel 14:25-26).

The scripture tells us that Absalom had good looks and even stood out in all of Israel, yet, he did David his father much harm.

Absalom told his servants to kill Amnon his brother (2 Samuel 13:29) he stole the hearts of the men of Israel (2 Samuel 15:1-6) and he slept with his father's concubines (2 Samuel 16:21-22).

Anyone would agree that Absalom though had very good looks did not have a good heart.

Man looks at the outside appearance but the Lord looks at the heart (1 Samuel 16:7).

Chapter Five

Warnings About the Heart

There are many reasons why the Lord tells us not to do certain things or expose ourselves to some things. We must remember that the Lord loves us and the instructions He tells us are for our own good.

The Bible tells us to guard our hearts with all diligence (Proverbs 4:23) for a reason.

Now, let us look at warnings about the heart:

Wrong Associations Can Affect the Heart

Have you ever met someone that you knew before and suddenly became hardened? You look further only to realize that the person has been hanging around the wrong people. The associations affected the heart of the person.

This is why we must be very careful with our associations.

Solomon is a good example of this in the Bible. The Lord had told him not to marry strange wives but he did not obey (1 Kings 11:1-3). At the end of his life, this is what was said of Solomon:

"*And he had seven hundred wives, princesses, and three hundred concubines; and his wives turned away his heart. [4] For it was so, when Solomon was old, that his wives turned his heart after other gods; and his heart was not [l] loyal to the Lord his God, as was the heart of his father David.*" (1 Kings 11:3-4).

Solomon's heart was affected to his detriment by his strange wives. What a costly price to pay!

Our Hearts Must Not be Overcharged with Cares of This Life

We must learn to cast our cares upon the Lord (1 Peter 5: 7) and be spiritually minded (Romans 8: 6). When we are spiritually minded, it will help us gain a heavenly perspective about issues that confront us.

The scripture is self-explanatory:

"*Heaven and earth shall pass away: but my words shall not pass away. And take heed to yourselves,* **lest at any time your hearts be overcharged with surfeiting, and drunkenness, and cares of this life, and so that day come upon you unawares.** *For as a snare shall it come on all them that dwell on the face of the whole earth.*" (Luke 21:33-35 KJV).

The good news is that we are not living this Christian walk in our own strength (Gal: 2:20).

We Must not be Deceived by Sin

According to scripture, we are dead to sin (1 Peter 2:24), therefore, a believer has no business living in sin.

We must maintain a tender heart and whenever we find that we have missed it, we must repent immediately and ask the Lord to forgive us.

"*But exhort one another daily, while it is called To day; lest any of you be hardened through the deceitfulness of sin*" (Hebrews 3:13 KJV).

We can see from the above scripture that sin can harden the heart which no believer can afford.

Backsliding is a Heart Matter

We have to focus on the goodness of God and the price that Jesus Christ our Lord has paid for us. We must guard our hearts with all diligence and be very careful what we expose our hearts to.

"The backslider in heart shall be filled with his own ways: and a good man shall be satisfied from himself." (Proverbs 14:14).

You can see from the above verse that backsliding is a heart condition that eventually will exhibit itself on the outside.

The Bible tells us to be fervent in spirit serving the Lord (Romans 12: 11).

The book of Hebrews also gives a warning about the heart.

"Take heed, brethren, lest there be in any of you an evil heart of unbelief, in departing from the living God." (Hebrews 3:12).

The Bible says that we should give no place to the devil (Ephesians 4:27).

So, how do we give no place to the devil in this matter? By guarding our hearts.

The Bible Warns Against Hardness of Heart

Hardening of the heart can have very severe consequences and this is one reason why we are instructed not to harden our hearts.

"Harden not your heart..." (Hebrews 3:8).

So, how does a person harden their heart? By refusing to respond to warnings, or convictions that they get through God's Word, the Holy Spirit, wise counsel, etc. By just being stubborn and refusing to apply their heart to instruction or things that they can learn from.

A good example of this is during the earthly ministry of the Lord, He asked His disciples, "Is your heart still hardened"?

This was in response to a statement that Jesus made and the disciples did not understand. Our Lord was telling them, "Did you not consider what I had done before"? The Lord has just multiplied bread for thousands, and shortly after that, the disciples were reasoning when Jesus spoke a parable that it was because they had not taken enough bread.

*"And He left them, and getting into the boat again, departed to the other side. 14 Now []the disciples had forgotten to take bread, and they did not have more than one loaf with them in the boat. 15 Then He charged them, saying, "Take heed, beware of the []leaven of the Pharisees and the leaven of Herod." 16 And they reasoned among themselves, saying, "It is because we have no bread." 17 But Jesus, being aware of it, said to them, "Why do you reason because you have no bread? Do you not yet perceive nor understand? **Is your heart []still hardened?** 18 Having*

eyes, do you not see? And having ears, do you not hear? And do you not remember? [19] *When I broke the five loaves for the five thousand, how many baskets full of fragments did you take up?" They said to Him, "Twelve."* [20] *"Also, when I broke the seven for the four thousand, how many large baskets full of fragments did you take up?" And they said, "Seven."* [21] *So He said to them, "How is it you do not understand?"* (Mark 8:13-21).

In other words, the disciples should have known better.

Unbelief can also cause the hardening of the heart.

This can be learned from the verse below after Jesus rose from the dead and some when told did not believe. Unbelief was also the reason why the children of Israel wandered in the wilderness for 40 years.

*"Later He appeared to the eleven as they sat at the table; and **He rebuked their unbelief** and **hardness of heart**, because they did not believe those who had seen Him after He had risen."* (Mark 16:14).

The children of Israel paid a heavy price for hardening their hearts and wandered in the wilderness for 40 years.

"While it is said, To day if ye will hear his voice, harden not your hearts, as in the provocation. [16] *For some, when they had heard, did provoke: howbeit not all that came out of Egypt by Moses.* [17] *But with whom was he grieved forty years? was it not with them that had sinned, whose carcases fell in the wilderness?* [18] *And to whom sware he that they should not enter into his rest, **but to them that believed not?*** [19] *So we see*

*that they **could not enter in because of unbelief.**"* (Hebrews 3:15-19 KJV).

The above scripture makes it clear that the reason why the children of Israel did not enter was because of unbelief which resulted in the hardening of the heart.

The Bible says that "all things are possible to him that believes." (Mark 9:23).

We must not allow the world or our temporary circumstances to lie to us.

Many of us are aware of Pharoah in the Bible. Despite all the signs, Pharoah refused to let the children of Israel go.

One of the signs that the Lord instructed Moses to do was to turn the rivers into blood (Exodus 7:20).

After this sign, there is a scripture that tells us one reason Pharoah's heart was hardened.

"Then Pharaoh turned and went into his house, and he did not take even this [divine sign] to *heart.*" (Exodus 7:23 AMP).

Pharoah did not set his heart on what happened to make the necessary adjustments.

Chapter Six

Our Hearts and our Walk with God

N ow that we know how important our hearts are in regard to our life and things we must avoid relating to the heart.

We have already stated that believing takes place in the heart (Romans 10: 10) and the importance of this in our Christian walk.

We have also mentioned in the previous chapter that our hearts are the soil for the Word of God. This is one reason we need to avoid arguments just before receiving the Word of God.

Have you ever driven to church with your family and on the way to service an argument starts in the car? During the service, instead of focusing on the Word of God, your mind is racing about what response you will give when you finish the service.

Could this be a plot of the enemy to cause a distraction? Of course, the enemy does not want to see you concentrate on the things of God. ***"The thief cometh not, but for to steal, and to kill, and to destroy:..."*** (John 10: 10a).

The Bible tells us to "give no place to the devil." (Ephesians 4:27). And looking at the parable of the sower, we can't afford the Word of God to fall by the wayside (Matthew 13: 4).

This is why we must prepare our hearts to receive the Word of God, and one way to do that is to avoid all forms of distractions in the first place.

Now, let us look at other functions of our hearts and our walk with the Lord.

We Must Allow God's Peace to Rule Our Hearts

The cares of this world come to us all. The Bible says that "In this world, you shall have tribulation" (John 16:33), nobody is exempted, however, one thing we can do is to allow God's peace to rule in our hearts.

"And let the peace of God rule in your hearts, to the which also ye are called in one body; and be ye thankful." (Colossians 3:15).

So, how do we allow God's peace to rule in our hearts?

It is simply by refusing to worry and by taking all our requests to the Lord in prayer and thanksgiving. This is the recipe for God's peace to guard our hearts and minds.

"Be anxious for nothing, but in everything by prayer and supplication, with thanksgiving, let your requests be made known to God; [7] and the peace of God, which surpasses all understanding, will guard your hearts and minds through Christ Jesus." (Philippians 4:6-7).

It is so important to allow God's peace to guard our hearts and minds. In today's world, as Christians, we must allow God's peace to guard our hearts and minds. A guard is a protection and this is what the peace of God will do for us.

Sanctify the Lord in our Hearts

Have you ever come across someone that loves the Lord passionately and is on fire for the Lord? Be rest assured that just the person has set the Lord apart in their hearts.

The scriptures say that we should "sanctify the Lord in our hearts" (1 Peter 3:15).

So, what does this mean?

We will look at the first part of this verse in a few translations.

"But sanctify the Lord God in your hearts." (1 Peter 3:15 KJV).

"But in your hearts set Christ apart [as holy—acknowledging Him, giving Him first place in your lives] as Lord." (1 Peter 3:15 AMP).

"But give reverent honor in your hearts to the Anointed One and treat him as the holy Master of your lives." (1 Peter 3:15 TPT).

Jesus Christ our Lord has done so much for us, the least we can do is give the Lord all of our hearts.

Making Melody to the Lord in our Hearts

We indeed are spirit beings and we can make melody in our hearts unto the Lord. We need to walk in the consciousness that we are walking with a living God and we are alive unto Him (Romans 6: 11).

*"And be not drunk with wine, wherein is excess; but be filled with the Spirit; Speaking to yourselves in psalms and hymns and spiritual songs, singing and **making melody in your heart to the Lord*** (Ephesians 5:18-19 KJV).

A True Heart with Full Assurance of Faith

We have mentioned in a previous chapter that believing takes place in the heart.

In the book of Hebrews, we are told to draw near to God with a true heart with full assurance of faith. In other words, our hearts should be full of faith.

*"**Let us draw near with a true heart in full assurance of faith**, having our hearts sprinkled from an evil conscience and our bodies washed with pure water. 23 Let us hold fast the confession of our hope without wavering, for He who promised is faithful)"* (Hebrews 10:21-23).

Do God's Will from the Heart

We have to remember that God sees the heart (Proverbs 21:2), and whatever we do for the Lord must be from the heart.

*"Servants, be obedient to them that are your masters according to the flesh, with fear and trembling, in singleness of your heart, as unto Christ; 6 Not with eyeservice, as menpleasers; but **as the servants of Christ, doing the will of God from the heart**; 7 With good will doing service, as to the Lord, and not to men."* (Ephesians 6:5-7 KJV).

While the above scripture is speaking to the relationship between servants and their masters, the principle of doing the will of God from the heart applies to all.

We can also find another scripture that echoes the same thing.

"And whatsoever ye do, do it heartily, as to the Lord, and not unto men." (Colossians 3:23).

Paul knew the importance of maintaining a good heart while sharing the gospel. He saw it as a privilege to be trusted by God to declare God's Word. This is what Paul said:

"But as we have been approved by God to be entrusted with the gospel, even so we speak, not as pleasing men, but God who tests our hearts." (1 Thess 2: 4).

Paul walked in the consciousness that God tries the hearts. In other words, God examines our hearts.

True Sacrifice is from the Heart

"The sacrifices of God *are* a broken spirit, A broken and a contrite heart—These, O God, You will not despise." (Psalms 51:17).

"The sacrifice you desire is a broken spirit. You will not reject a broken and repentant heart, O God." (Psalms 51:17 NLT).

We have to be intentional about having a contrite heart. Contrite means a recognition that one has done wrong and is repentant.

Psalms 51 was written by David after he sinned against the Lord in the matter of Bathsheba. David's heart was truly repentant.

Giving Should be From the Heart

Have you ever sat in a place and felt pressured to give? Well, according to scripture, we should decide what to give from the heart and then give. We should not feel obligated to give if it is not from the heart.

"But this I say, He which soweth sparingly shall reap also sparingly; and he which soweth bountifully shall reap also bountifully. **Every man according as he purposeth in his heart,** *so let him give; not grudg-*

ingly, or of necessity: for God loveth a cheerful giver." (2 Corinthians 9:6-7 KJV).

From the above scripture, our giving should be a direct response to what is in our hearts.

It is Our Hearts That Trust in the Lord

It is our hearts that trust in the Lord; this is one reason why we must guard our hearts. We must not have idols in our hearts that exalt themselves against the Lord in our hearts.

Therefore, our hearts must be focused on the Lord.

While we honor those before us, the Lord must take the utmost and first priority in our hearts.

*"The Lord is my strength and my shield; **My heart trusted in Him**, and I am helped; Therefore my heart greatly rejoices, And with my song I will praise Him."* (Psalms 28:7).

Chapter Seven

The Importance of a Pure Heart

In the previous chapter, we looked at different types of hearts. Now, we are going to look into the importance of having a pure heart in a bit more detail.

Do you want to see God?

One criterion is to have a pure heart.

"Blessed are the pure in heart: for they shall see God." (Matthew 5: 8).

*"Who shall ascend into the hill of the Lord? or who shall stand in his holy place? He that hath clean hands, **and a pure heart**; who hath not lifted up his soul unto vanity, nor sworn deceitfully."* (Psalms 24:3-4 KJV).

So, what does it mean to have a pure heart?

It means having no hidden agendas, no wrong motives, and dealing with God and man with a clean heart.

Nobody can fool God because God sees and tries the hearts (Proverbs 21: 2 & Proverbs 17: 3).

Therefore, isn't it wise to maintain a right and pure heart before the Lord?

Have you ever come across someone that you thought was a friend or acquaintance? Only to find out that such a person had a motive. Immediately they get what they want they are gone or suddenly change.

People with pure hearts do not behave in such ways.

We are to call upon the Lord from out of a pure heart (2 Timothy 2:22).

The Bible also tells us to love one another out of a pure heart.

"Since you have purified your souls in obeying the truth [] through the Spirit in [] sincere love of the brethren, love one another fervently with a pure heart." (1 Peter 1: 22).

How would this look like if we did love one another fervently with a pure heart? They would be no one trying to take advantage of another, nobody trying to help and connect with someone for a wrong motive.

A pure heart is a standard by which we are to relate to God and man according to scripture.

The Bible also tells us that the words of the pure are pleasant words (Proverbs 15:26). And why? Because such words will come from a pure heart.

Sometimes, our words can reflect the state of our hearts.

Chapter Eight

The Importance of a Tender Heart

A person with a tender heart will act accordingly and respond when they hear God's Word or any positive correction.

A person with a tender heart will also be quick to repent and apologize to those that they offend. Being tender-hearted is for our own good because it will allow God's mercy to speak for us.

A good example of this can be found in the book of 2 Kings when Josiah heard the evil that was to come upon the land. The whole account can be found in (2 Kings 22- 1-20).

The rewards of his tender heart can be found in these scriptures:

"But as for the king of Judah, who sent you to inquire of the Lord, in this manner you shall speak to him, 'Thus says the Lord God of Israel: "Concerning the words which you have heard— **¹⁹ because your heart**

was tender, and you humbled yourself before the Lord when you heard what I spoke against this place *and against its inhabitants, that they would become a desolation and a curse, and you tore your clothes and wept before Me, I also have heard you," says the Lord.* **20** *"Surely, therefore, I will* [ ]*gather you to your fathers, and you shall* [ ]*be gathered to your grave in peace; and* ***your eyes shall not see all the calamity which I will bring on this place."*** *So they brought back word to the king."* (2 Kings 22:18- 20).

That's simply amazing! Josiah did not see the evil to come because his heart was tender.

We can see from the above scripture how a tender heart connects us to the mercy of God.

So, how do we cultivate a tender heart? By meditating on the word of God and acting on corrections the Lord brings our way, by quickly repenting when we know that we have done wrong, dropping things and forgiving others quickly, being quick to say sorry or apologize even if it seems you are the only one doing it in a relationship.

Being tender-hearted has many benefits. It's Christ-like to be tender-hearted. When we do wrong, God wants us to repent so He can have mercy on us.

Chapter Nine

Health Care for the Heart

Now that we are aware of the importance of our hearts, what can we do to ensure that we maintain an upright heart?

One thing is certain, we must be intentional about what we apply our hearts to.

According to the scripture, we must apply our hearts to:

Instruction   (Proverbs 23:12)

Understanding (Proverbs 2:2).

Knowledge   (Proverbs 22:17).

And we must guard our hearts with all diligence (Proverbs 4:23).

If we were to guard our house, what would we do? We would be vigilant about what we allow into our houses. The same principle applies to our hearts.

We must also spend time in the presence of the Lord and soak our hearts in His presence.

Chapter Ten

Prayers for the Heart

Now that we know how important the heart is with our walk with the Lord and relating to others, there are some prayers we can pray that can help us.

"And the Lord direct your hearts into the love of God, and into the patient waiting for Christ." (2 Thess 3:5 KJV).

When our hearts are focused on the love of God, how God loves mankind, and also our hearts focus on the return of Christ this will influence the way we conduct our lives.

Could this be the reason Paul prayed this prayer?

What we think about in our hearts is so important. This is why David prayed:

"Let the words of my mouth and the meditation of my heartBe accept-able in Your sight, O Lord, my [] strength and my Redeemer." (Psalms 19:14).

We can ask the Lord to strengthen our hearts (Psalms 31:24).

Chapter Eleven

Conclusion

The state of our hearts is such a priority to the Lord that His eyes are looking throughout the earth to show Himself strong on behalf of those whose hearts are perfect towards Him (2 Chronicles 16:9).

The Lord is not looking for the richest, the smartest, the most handsome, or beautiful but those whose hearts are perfect towards Him.

Therefore, what the Lord is looking for anyone can achieve because it does not cost anything materially to have a good and upright heart.

Will you be that person?

As Christians, we have the added advantage that our hearts have already been purged by the blood of Jesus (Hebrews 10:22), and the love of God has been poured into our hearts by the Holy Spirit given unto us (Romans 5:5).

At the end of it all, one thing that the Lord will judge will be the intents of our hearts.

"Therefore judge nothing before the time, until the Lord comes, who will both bring to light the hidden things of darkness and reveal the [] counsels of the hearts. Then each one's praise will come from God." (1 Corinthians 4:5).

Having a good and upright heart is not automatic otherwise having a meek and quiet spirit would not be of great price in the eyes of the Lord (1 Peter 3:4).

The good news is that the Lord will not tell us to do what we cannot do.

Our hearts are so important that one thing that Lord promised in the Old Testament was to give them a heart of flesh so that they serve Him (Ezekiel 11:19-20). The Lord also said that He would put His fear in their hearts so that they do not depart from Him (Jeremiah 32:40).

Under the New Covenant, the Lord said that He would put His laws into our hearts and minds (Hebrews 10:16).

Why?

Because our hearts are the main source of our walk with God.

Now that we know how important our hearts are, we must be intentional about guarding our hearts with all diligence.

We must take responsibility for what we hear and pay attention to. If we hear something that affects our hearts negatively, we need to protect our hearts and avoid such an influence on us.

For out of the heart are the issues of life (Proverbs 4:23).

Salvation Prayer

F ather God, I come to you in Jesus' name. I admit that I am a sinner, and I now receive the sacrifice that Jesus Christ paid for me.

I confess with my mouth the Lord Jesus, and I believe in my heart that God raised Him from the dead.

I now declare that Jesus Christ is my Lord and Saviour.

Thank you, Father, for saving me in Jesus' name.

I am now your child. Amen.

If you've said this prayer for the first time, send an email to Bisiwrite r@gmail.com . Start reading your Bible and ask the Lord to guide you to a good church.

About Author

Bisi Oladipupo has been a Christian for many years and lives in the United Kingdom with her family.

Bisi attended a few Bible colleges, and she has completed a diploma in Biblical Studies from a UK Bible college.

She is a teacher of God's Word, coordinates Bible studies, and has a YouTube channel at https://www.youtube.com/c/BisiOladipupo123.

Her author page is www.bisiwriter.com

She writes regularly, and her blog website is www.inspiredwords.org

You can contact Bisi by email at bisiwriter@gmail.com

Books Also By Bisi

1. The Twelve Apostles of Jesus Christ: Lessons We Can Learn

2. The Lord's Cup in Communion: The Significance of taking the Lord's Supper

3. Different Ways to Receive Healing from Scripture and Walk in Health

4. Believing on The Name of Jesus Christ: What Every Believer Needs to Know

5. The Mind and Your Christian Walk: The Impact of the mind on our Christian walk

6. Relationship Skills in the Bible: Scriptural Principles of relating to others

7. The Nature of God's Kingdom: The Characteristics of the Kingdom of God

8. The Person of the Holy Spirit

Afterword

If you enjoyed this book, please take a few moments to write a review of it. Thank you!